HE IS BORN
EMMANUEL!

A CHRISTMAS PRESENTATION OF 5 SONGS IN UNISON/2-PART

CREATED BY MARTY PARKS

Performance Time: 17 minutes

Copyright © 2010 by Lillenas Publishing Company, Box 419527, Kansas City, MO 64141.

All scripture qoutations are from the *Holy Bible, New International Version*® (NIV®).
Copyright © 1973, 1978, 1984 by International Bible Society.
Used by permission of Zondervan Publishing House. All rights reserved.

lillenas.com

Contents

Jesus, Our Emmanuel *with* Let All Mortal Flesh Keep Silence   3

Before the Starry Universe   13

The Birthday of a King *with* He Is Born, Alleluia   20

Infinite Lord   27

Gloria *with* Angels We Have Heard on High   32

Jesus, Our Emmanuel

with
Let All Mortal Flesh Keep Silence

Words and Music by
MARTY PARKS
Arr. by Marty Parks

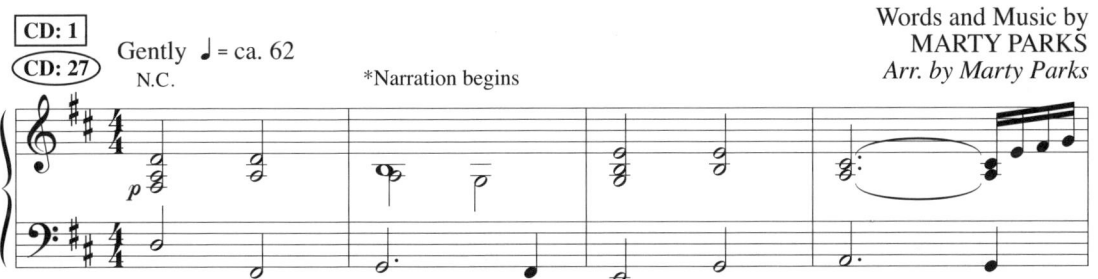

NARRATOR: This is the story of Christmas– a story so dramatic, so unthinkable that only God could have imagined it. Only God could have initiated and fulfilled it. Only God could have loved this much.

And so, He did just that. With heaven's armies watching
– speechless, in hushed amazement
– God Himself filled our deepest need . . . with Himself.

Copyright © 2001 by PsalmSinger Music (BMI). All rights reserved.
Administered by The Copyright Company, PO Box 128139,
Nashville, TN 37212-8139. CCLI #3308017

PLEASE NOTE: Copying of this product is NOT covered by CCLI licenses. For CCLI information call 1-800-234-2446.

Before the Starry Universe

KEN BIBLE

Traditional English Carol
Arr. by Marty Parks

Boldly ♩ = ca. 80
N.C.

CHOIR *unis.*,
with wonder

Be-fore the star-ry u-ni-verse there reigned the Great I

Copyright © 2003 by LNWhymns.com (ASCAP). All rights reserved.
Administered by The Copyright Company, PO Box 128139,
Nashville, TN 37212-8139. CCLI #3980954

PLEASE NOTE: Copying of this product is NOT covered by CCLI licenses. For CCLI information call 1-800-234-2446.

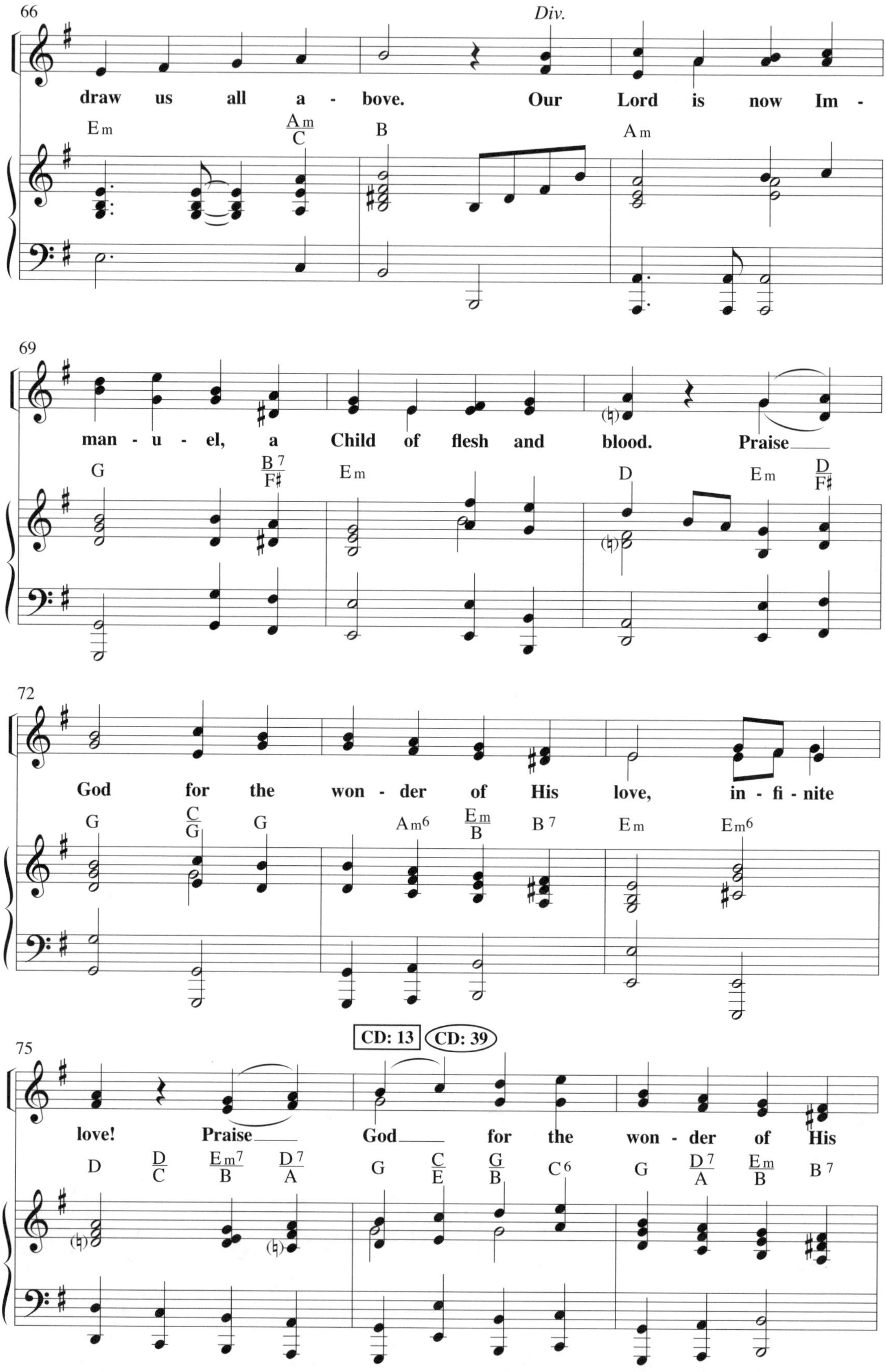
66
Div.
draw us all a - bove. Our Lord is now Im -
Em
Am/C
B
Am
69
man - u - el, a Child of flesh and blood. Praise
G
B7/F♯
Em
D
Em
D/F♯
72
God for the won - der of His love, in - fi - nite
G
C/G
G
Am6
Em/B
B7
Em
Em6
CD: 13
CD: 39
75
love! Praise God for the won - der of His
D
D/C
Em7/B
D7/A
G
C/E
G/B
C6
G
D7/A
Em/B
B7

NARRATOR *(without music)*: The mystery of the incarnation is beyond our understanding. It's broader than our imagination and it's outside the scope of our experience. The presence of God has always evoked wonder and delight; reverence and fear.

God was about to change our world in a startling way. A new day was dawning. A new age was being ushered in, the likes of which we'd never seen before. *(Music begins)* Suddenly, the whole earth was an unwitting host to the presence of God Himself . . . God with us.

The Birthday of a King

with
He Is Born, Alleluia

Words and Music by
W. H. NEIDLINGER
Arr. by Marty Parks

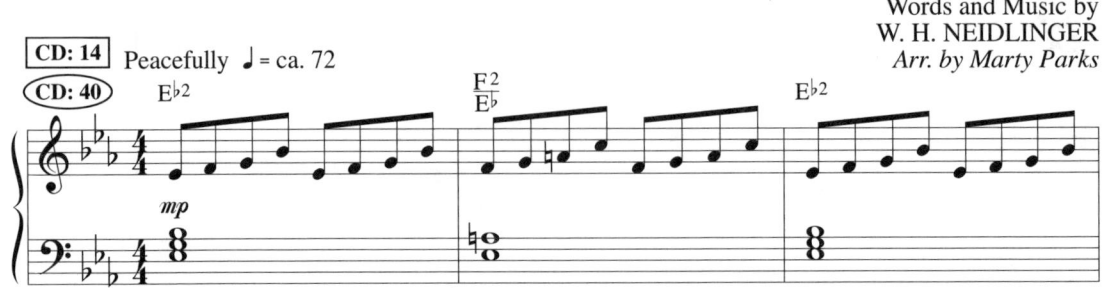

*Words and Music by MARTY PARKS. Copyright © 2006 by PsalmSinger Music (BMI). All rights reserved. Administered by The Copyright Company, PO Box 128139, Nashville, TN 37212-8139. CCLI #4918664

Arr. © 2006 by PsalmSinger Music (BMI).
All rights reserved. Administered by The Copyright Company,
PO Box 128139, Nashville, TN 37212-8139. CCLI #4950392

Do Not Photocopy

PLEASE NOTE: Copying of this product is NOT covered by CCLI licenses. For CCLI information call 1-800-234-2446.

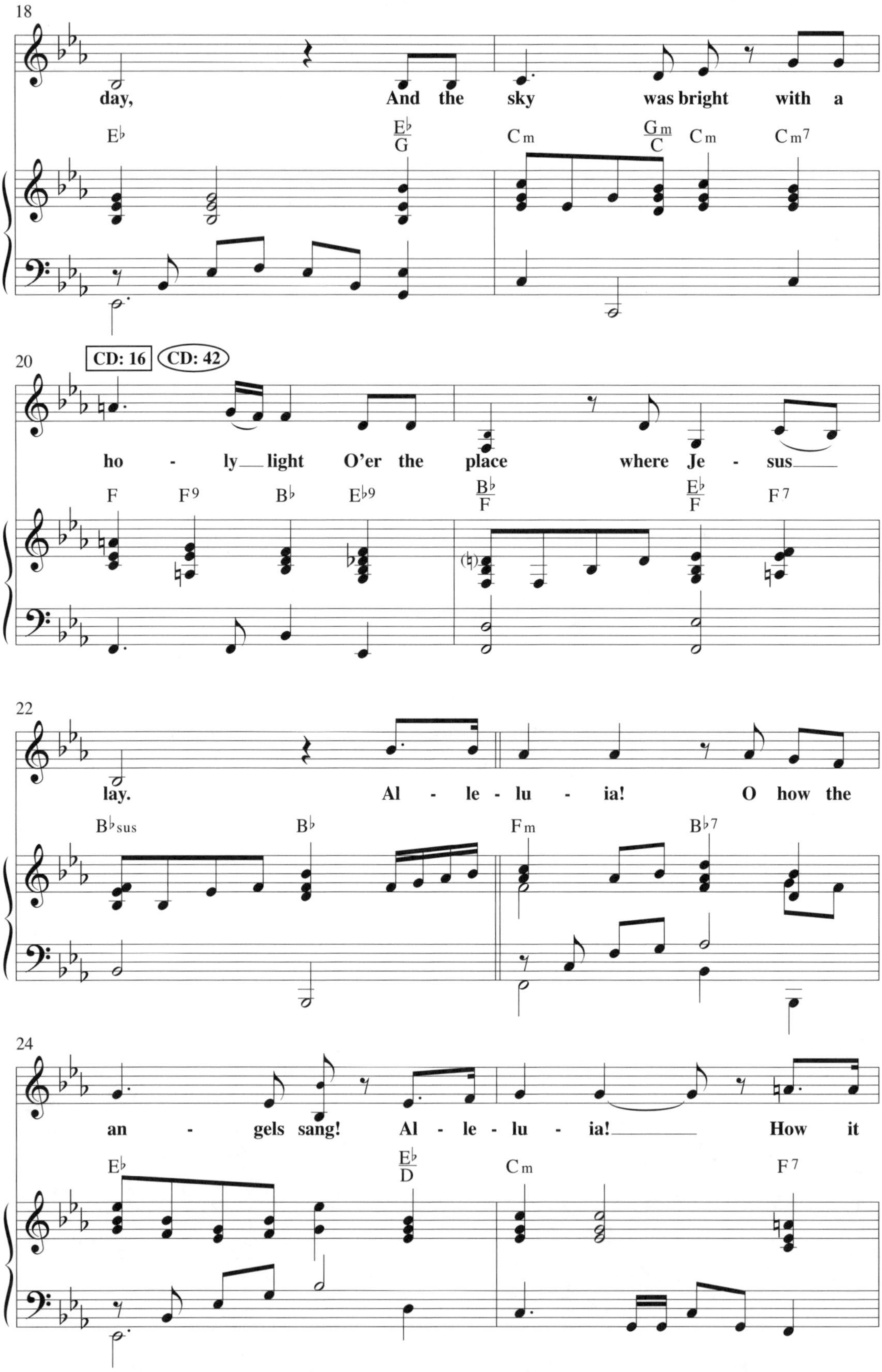
18
day, And the sky was bright with a
E♭ E♭/G Cm Gm/C Cm Cm7
20
CD: 16
CD: 42
ho - ly light O'er the place where Je - sus
F F9 B♭ E♭9 B♭/F E♭/F F7
22
lay. Al - le - lu - ia! O how the
B♭sus B♭ Fm B♭7
24
an - gels sang! Al - le - lu - ia! How it
E♭ E♭/D Cm F7

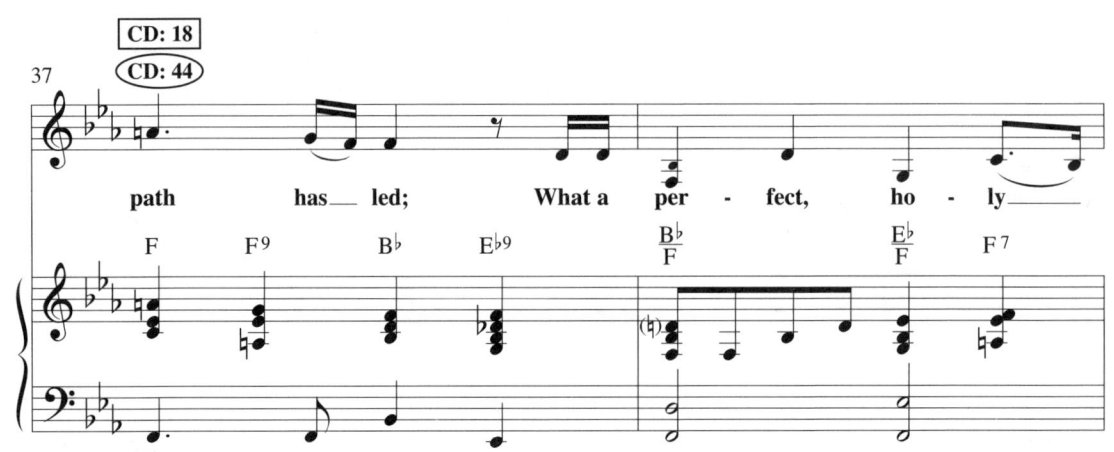
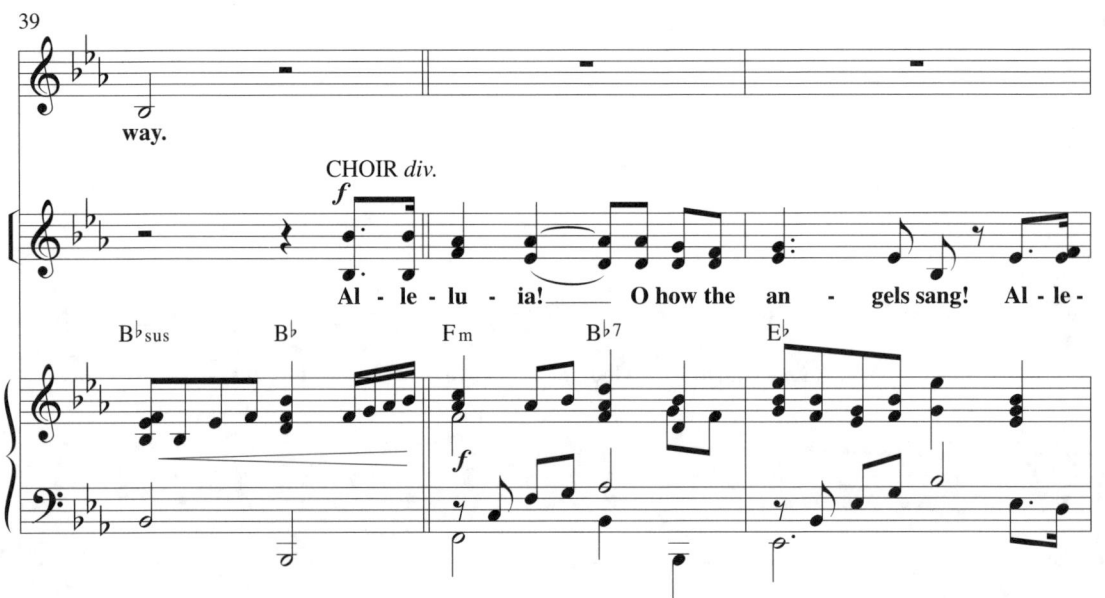

Infinite Lord

KEN BIBLE

Traditional English Melody
Arr. by Marty Parks

Quietly ♩ = ca. 78

NARRATOR *(before music begins):* How totally like God to surprise us with His coming. *(Music begins)* He filled the earth with the glory of His presence, but announced His arrival in unexpected ways. Oh, there had been signs and prophecies all along. But when He finally appeared, only a handful even noticed. A group of shepherds, outcasts really, were assured that to them a Savior had been born. And a very knowledgeable group of seekers were led on an amazing journey by a single mysterious star.

What they found was a Child looking much like themselves; a flesh and blood Messiah wrapped up in meekness and clothed in humility. The infinite as a mortal, a Savior in swaddling clothes.

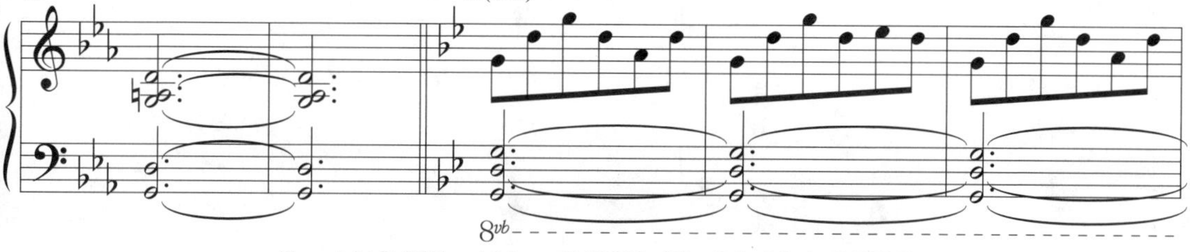

Copyright © 1991 and this arr. © 2006 by Pilot Point Music (ASCAP).
All rights reserved. Administered by The Copyright Company,
PO Box 128139, Nashville, TN 37212-8139. CCLI #2350372

Do Not Photocopy

PLEASE NOTE: Copying of this product is NOT covered by CCLI licenses. For CCLI information call **1-800-234-2446.**

NARRATOR *(without music)*: And so, He came. Christ, the Messiah, the Promised One. He came to us . . . as one of us . . . so that we might become His children, His beloved, His very own.

And that's the story of Christmas. Only God could have loved this much. Only God could have responded to our need in such an extravagant way that the angels– once silenced in awe and wonder– would erupt and fill the heavens with their own exclamation of praise.

(Music begins)
And their song has become our song: Glory! Glory to God in the highest!

Gloria
with
Angels We Have Heard on High

Traditional

ANTONIO VIVALDI
Arr. by Marty Parks

Arr. © 2003 by PsalmSinger Music (BMI). All rights reserved.
Administered by The Copyright Company, PO Box 128139,
Nashville, TN 37212-8139. CCLI #4038135

PLEASE NOTE: Copying of this product is NOT covered by CCLI licenses. For CCLI information call 1-800-234-2446.

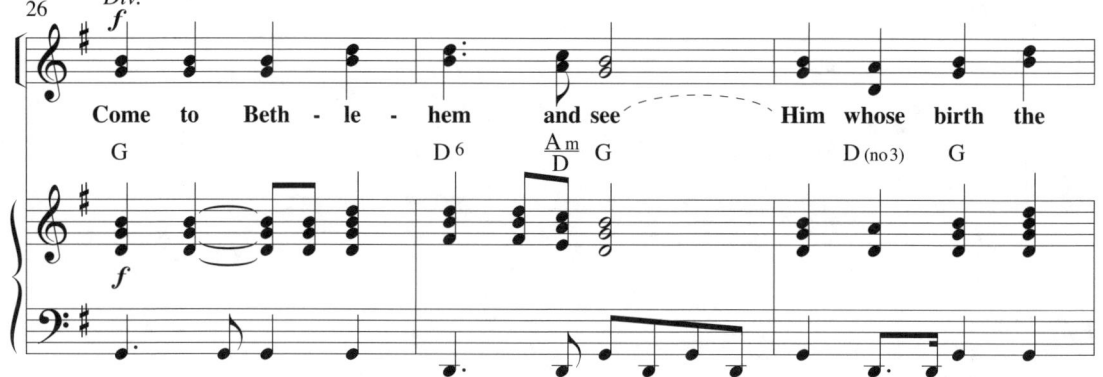